GROWING
FRUIT

Tracy Nelson Maurer

GREEN THUMB GUIDES

The Rourke Book Company, Inc.
Vero Beach, Florida 32964

Tracy Nelson Maurer specializes in nonfiction and business writing. Her most recently published children's books include the Bodyworks series, also from Rourke Publishing. A graduate of the University of Minnesota Journalism School, Tracy lives with her husband Mike and two children in Superior, Wisconsin.

With appreciation to gardeners Lois M. Nelson, Harvey Almstedt, and Lois I. Nelson; and to Richard J. Zondag, Jung Seed Company.

PHOTO CREDITS:
All photos and illustrations © East Coast Studios except p. 12 and p. 13 © Corel

PRODUCED & DESIGNED by East Coast Studios
eastcoaststudios.com

EDITORIAL SERVICES:
Lois M. Nelson
Pamela Schroeder

Library of Congress Cataloging-in-Publication Data

Maurer, Tracy, 1965-
    Growing fruit / Tracy Nelson Maurer.
      p. cm. — (Green thumb guides)
    Includes bibliographical references (p.).
    Summary: Describes how to plant, care for, prune, and protect various kinds of fruit.
    ISBN 1-55916-252-X
    1. Fruit—culture—Juvenile literature. 2. Fruit—Juvenile literature. [1. Fruit.] I. Title.

SB357.2 .M38 2000
634—dc21
                                                            00–026922

Printed in the USA

Table of Contents

Sweet Treats

Strawberries and cream, apple juice, blueberry pie, bananas—many sweet things to eat and drink come from fruit. Fruit grows on trees and shrubs. Plants that live for only one season, called **annuals** (AN you ulz), also grow fruit.

Botanists, scientists who study plants, say that fruit is the part of a plant that holds seeds. Some seeds are large, like the pits in peaches or cherries. Others are tiny, such as the little seeds on a strawberry.

Fun Fact
Tomato is a fruit because it holds the plant's seeds. Usually, fruits not eaten for desserts are called vegetables.

Fruit tastes good and it's good for you! You should eat fruit every day for a healthy body.

Growing Fruit

Gardeners grow fruit everywhere. Most fruit trees grow to about 25 feet (7.6 meters) tall. They fit in a city yard or a country farm. Orchards stretch as far as you can see with rows of apples, oranges, peaches, or other fruit.

Rows of orange trees fill this orchard, or fruit tree farm.

Blueberry plants are about three years old before they grow fruit. One plant can give you two to four quarts of blueberries each year for up to 40 years!

Growing your own fruit takes more care, planning, and time than other types of gardening. Before you begin, ask an adult for help. Read other gardening books or check the Internet to learn about your favorite fruit. Your plants will reward your work with sweet pickings!

Pick Your Fruit

Every fruit plant likes a certain **climate** (KLIH mit). Some like cold winters. Some don't. **Citrus** (SI truss) plants, such as orange trees and grapefruit trees, grow only where it stays above freezing.

Many fruit plants need lots of space. One watermelon seed can become a long vine with huge fruit weighing up to 100 pounds! Some strawberries, dwarf orange trees, and other special small fruits will grow in pots.

Learn what your fruit plant likes best—cold or warm, wet or dry, sun or shade. Draw your yard on paper. Talk with an adult about where to plant.

Pineapples need a lot of room to grow. Most fruit plants do. A watermelon vine can grow longer than six feet. That's about the size of a grown man.

Planting Fruit

Try growing watermelon or cantaloupe from seeds. Did you know these two fruits come from the cucumber family? Start your seeds indoors early in the spring. This gives your watermelon and cantaloupe a longer growing season.

Instead of sowing seeds, you may want to buy small plants called seedlings from a garden center or nursery. Look for strong, leafy, and dark green berry plants, shrubs, or trees to bring home.

Strawberry plants like this make a good choice for new fruit gardeners. Apple trees, raspberry shrubs, and watermelon are also easy to grow.

Welcome, Bees!

Listen to an apple tree in bloom. A buzz fills the air! Hungry bees drink the sweet nectar inside the blossoms, or flowers.

A powder called pollen sticks to the bees. Pollen rubs off when the bees stop at the next blossom. Bees help spread pollen from blossom to blossom and from tree to tree.

Most plants need bees to help spread pollen.

Bees also carry pollen to their hives for food.

Apple blossoms need pollen from other apple blossoms or they cannot grow into fruit. Gardeners usually plant at least two of every fruit to help mix the pollen.

Fun Fact

Honeybees work 12 hours a day. They gather pollen and nectar from about 8:00 in the morning until 8:00 at night. They bring pollen to the hive for baby bee food.

Tending Fruit Plants

Gardeners must care for, or tend, their fruit plants. They make sure the plants get about 1 inch (2.5 centimeters) of water each week.

Fruit plants also need special food called **fertilizer** (FUR tuh LIE zur). Old kitchen scraps soaked in water or well-rotted cow droppings make good fertilizer.

Some plants need extra food. Watermelons take a lot from the soil. When they stop growing, they leave very little food behind for next year's plants. Ask an expert about the right fertilizer for your fruit.

Start your small plants indoors in soil you buy from the store. Do not use soil from your garden or yard, since this soil may have bugs.

Pruning Woody Plants

Fruit trees and shrubs are woody plants. They need a trim, or **pruning** (PROON ing), every year to stay healthy and strong. Ask an adult to cut off dead or broken branches.

Some plants grow more fruit when you prune in spring. Others do better when you prune in fall. An expert can tell you when to prune.

It is also important to spread **mulch** (MULCH) under your fruit plants. A layer about two inches deep of small wood chips, bark chips, or pine needles helps keep water in and weeds out. A blanket of straw over strawberries protects them from harsh winters.

Fun Fact
Some citrus trees grow up to 1,000 pounds of fruit each year!

Check with an expert before you prune, or cut, a fruit tree. You don't want to cut off next year's fruit buds!

Guard Against Pests

Do you love to eat fresh fruit? You're not alone. All kinds of bugs also enjoy eating fruit plants! Brown spots, holes, or droopy leaves often mean insect pests came for dinner. Mice, rabbits, and deer also nibble on plants, shrubs, or trees.

Wire fences around these plants help to keep out mice, rabbits, and deer. Ask an expert about other ways to stop pests from eating your fruit plants.

All kinds of pests eat fruit plants. Some bugs eat seeds, stems, or leaves. Others eat roots. A few pests wait for ripe fruit.

Rotting fruit brings pests. **Harvest** (HAHR vist) all the fruit every season to keep pests away. You can also wrap sticky tape, wire fence, or tubes around woody fruit plants to keep animals and insects away. Talk to an expert about other ways to stop pests.

Fun Fact

Gardeners often build houses for birds, bats, and frogs to keep away pests. These animals eat millions of insects and insect eggs. One bat can eat 1,200 insects in an hour!

Heaping Harvests

Watch people in grocery stores. They tap, squeeze, and sniff the fruit to see if it is ripe. Gardeners also check their fruit to know when to harvest. A dull, hollow sound when you knock on a watermelon means it's time to harvest. Read books, save seed packages, and ask adults for help.

Harvest the fruit gently. Lift and twist fruit off trees. Pull raspberries clean off the white core. Leave the stem on strawberries. Place each one softly in a bucket out of the sun.

Enjoy the fruit of your labor!

Gardeners enjoy sharing their harvests.

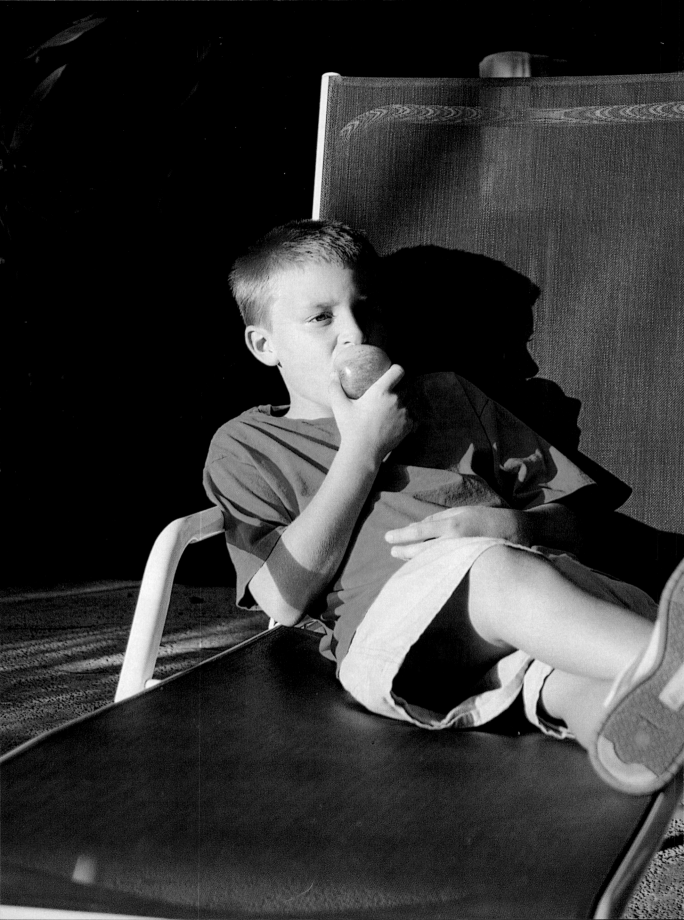

GLOSSARY

annuals (AN you ulz) — plants that grow for one season and die in the fall

citrus (SI truss) — a group of fruit trees and shrubs, such as grapefruit, lemon, and orange, that grow best in warm climates

climate (KLIH mit) — the normal weather for an area, including how hot or cold it gets and how much rain falls

fertilizer (FUR tuh LIE zur) — food for plants that gardeners add to the soil

harvest (HAHR vist) — to pick or gather the fruit from plants

mulch (MULCH) — the wood chips, pine needles, or other covers, spread on the ground

pruning (PROON ing) — cutting off branches, especially dead or broken branches

Gardeners say that fruit grown at home tastes better than fruit from a store. What do you think?

INDEX

FURTHER READING

Find out more about gardening with these helpful books:

• Ambler, Wayne et al. *Treasury of Gardening.* Lincolnwood, Ill.: Publications International, 1994.

• Hart, Avery, and Paul Mantell. *Kids Garden!: The Anytime, Anyplace Guide To Sowing & Growing Fun.* Charlotte, Vermont: Williamson Publishing Co., 1996.

• *Rodale's Illustrated Encyclopedia of Gardening and Landscaping Techniques.* Edited by Barbara W. Ellis. Emmaus, Penn.: Rodale Press, 1990.

On-line resources:

Search for "kids gardening" on the World Wide Web to see many different sites.

• www.garden.org (c) National Gardening Association, 1999.

• www.letsfindout.com (c) Knowledge Adventure, 1998.

• members.aol.com/bats4kids (c) bats4kids